To Boldly Go

Yes You Can Boldly Go And Change Your Life by Starting A Business Today

Another book in the Yes I Can Book Series

Written by

Marc E. Parham

1	CAPTAINS LOG, STAR DATE – TODAY!	3
2	TO BOLDLY GO	6
3	LIVE LONG AND PROSPER	7
4	I'M A DOCTOR, NOT A…	10
5	MAKE IT SO	13
6	TO BOLDLY GO WHERE NO MAN HAS GONE BEFORE	18
7	SULU, SET PHASERS TO STUN	21
8	WARP FACTOR 7	24
9	HIGHLY ILLOGICAL…	28
10	I'M GIVIN' HER ALL SHE'S GOT, CAPTAIN!"	34
11	THE FINAL FRONTIER	36
12	SUMMARY	38
13	CAPBUILDER SELF-ASSESSMENT	39
14	CAPBUILDER BUSINESS IDEA EVALUATION TOOL	44
15	CAPBUILDER COACHING PROGRAMS	54
16	ABOUT THE AUTHOR	57
17	CAPBUILDER RESOURCE PAGE	59

1 Captains Log, Star Date – Today!

My name is Marc Parham. I have been working for over 25 years as a business coach to help people change their lives by starting and growing their own small business.

I am a small business expert, author and host of the CAPBuilder Talk radio show. www.capbuildertalk.com

I have been a business owner for over 30 years where I experienced first hand the success and failures of this world of small business.

In 2013 I was invited to the White House to meet personally with President Obama to give council on how the pending government shut down was going to affect small business.

The one interesting fact that I have found while working with people all over the world is that most people have everything it takes to start their own business but the only thing is,

They Don't Know They Can!

Most people have not been trained to think and work for themselves. From the day we were born we were told what to do, when to do it, how to do it regardless of our age or our status in life. Even more important we allowed our lives to be guided by others. It is not our fault.

To fit in, we had to fit in!

I wrote this book called "To Boldly Go" because this exactly what you must do if you want to change your life.

You must Boldy Go where you have never been before....

My goal with this book is to give you something that you can use to begin to create a plan for yourself to change your life. This book will provide discussion and suggestions on things to do that worked for me help me change my life.

I've created great easy to use coaching programs that will help you work through what you need to do to take control of your life. You can go to www.capbuildermember.com to signup to become a member of the CAPBuilder Network to have access to our great coaching resources.

My mission is not only to tell you how but to also equip you with the tools to make the changes necessary for you to live your purposed life.

After each chapter, there will be a reference to the respective coaching program that may be associated with the chapter. You may select the coaching program and your method of study.

My suggestion is that you read the book completely first and then come back and select the coaching program that you want to take.

If you need assistance I am always a click away. You may schedule a coaching session with me by going to www.meetwithmarc.com and suggest a time for us to get together and I will respond with a confirmation. I can coach you by video conference, phone or face to face. It does not matter where you are!

2 To Boldly Go

> *"Our mission is to explore strange new worlds, seek out new life, new civilizations, to boldly go where no man has gone before"*

Yes, I am, and will always be a "treekie". I realize now, that the appeal of the show Star Trek was that it helped me to realize that there was more to life than what was going on around us. It was multicultural, they were explorers working together to learn about not only themselves but the worlds around them. It helped me to believe that anything was possible as long as you were willing to escape from the norm and step outside of your comfort zone.

People say you should live outside the box. I have always said "What Box?"

If you believe that the box is there, guess what? There it will be! It truly amazes me how powerful our minds are. Our thoughts can keep us from achieving the goals that we set for ourselves.

What's even more amazing is that the thoughts of others can also keep us for these same goals. We have been conditioned to listen to others on how to run our life (*more on this later*).

Are you living in a box?

3   Live Long and Prosper

> "***prosper*** is a verb that **means** to make steady progress. As any fan of Star Trek knows, "**live long and prosper**" is good advice. The verb **prosper means** to do well, to succeed, or thrive."

Would an additional $250 to $500 a month change your life? Many people think that you must start a business that makes a lot of money. Of course, this would be nice but it takes a lot of time and effort to do this. It may be that you are not ready to do it today. What about if you start a business, doing something that you truly enjoy, and you make additional revenue for your household and family?

Most of the time we have skills that people will pay us for. We never looked at it like having a business. Are you the person that everyone calls on when they need help with something? Maybe help putting together an event, or helping someone move, help someone paint or fix their house. These are all skills that you could possibly start a business around.

We think that sometimes because it's for a friend or something we enjoy doing that we should not make any money with it. There are many people that have turned their hobbies into very successful businesses. Of course, not everything we may do, will be to make money. Some of you may decide to do things to change the lives of others. It's up to you to determine the value of your own time.

One thing that is most important, is that you decide to do something. We all have something that we are purposed to do. It is just that some of us never get the opportunity to realize it. There are some of us that realize it but never take actions to make it happen. There are many reasons. The fear success, fear of failure and sometimes just the fear of getting started. It has come to the point however that we must set fear side and take action, not just action but massive action.

When we do this, we must give it everything we have to make it happen. I want you to start doing research on people that have taken simple ideas and turned them in the businesses that have change the world as we know it today. You will find that there are many people that took something as simple as making candles and have turned it into million-dollar businesses.

There are many reasons that people start home-based businesses. Some enjoy the flexibility of working hours. Others enjoy doing their own thing. Most would agree the tax benefits are amazing. Whatever the reason, you must find the one that works for you. I mean, really works for you.

One mistake that most people make is they just jump out there and try it. They try one idea after another without fully investigating if that idea is going to work for them. They never actually put together a plan. They end up using money, time and sometimes relationships with their friends and supporters.

That's why it's important that regardless of what you decide to do, you develop a plan to do it. A plan is going to be the most critical factor in your success. It does not have to be that 25-page monster that we all fear. You can put together plan on one page. Your plan doesn't have to be big or overly detailed but it does have to be!

DoThis! – Create Your Personal Plan. Go to http://www.capbuildermember.com and select the **Personal Development Coaching Program**.

4 I'M A DOCTOR, NOT A...

> *"Knowing why you are is your purpose. Knowing who you are is your style. Knowing what you are is your character"* — **Debasish Mridha**

Who are you today? I mean right now! For a lot of us we've been so busy being who others wanted us to be, we are not quite sure who we are. This is not a bad thing, this is a life thing. We've been husbands, we've been wives, sisters and brothers. We've been just about anybody that we needed to be to fit into the world we live.

It is time that we decided who we want to be. Not only decide who we want to be but also working hard to become that person.

Do you know who you are?

The success that you have in life is closely linked to having an interest in the things you do to live your life. Involvement with activities in which you are interested in can make it easier to become successful. Think about the task that bring you pleasure. Think about some of your current successes. Make a list of your accomplishments and the things you do well in something you derived a great sense of pride, achievement, and satisfaction.

No, we can't like everything that happens to us but we can definitely make an effort to involve ourselves in activities that bring us the most pleasure.

That is of course, if we figure out what those are based on who we are today. Who are we at this very moment? Not who we were, not who we want to be, who we are right now!

Self-Assessment

Self-assessment involves examining your interest, values, personality, and skills. When your life choices are in line with your interests, values, personality, and skills you will be much happier more productive.

A few questions to ask yourself:

- In what areas of my life do people compliment and give me praise or recognition?
- Do I enjoy activities that involve people, things, or information?
- Do I prefer a regular routine or a schedule that changes quite frequently?
- Do I prefer to work as part of a team or work alone or with small groups of people?
- I prefer to lead or follow?
- Do I like to communicate in writing, verbally, or visually?
- Do I enjoy creative activities?
- How important his work life balance to me?

These are just a few of the questions you need to ask yourself. There are several online self-assessments that you can do at your leisure. I suggest you look up and find one that works for you then do it. Find one that asks the questions that are the most important to you.

DoThis! – Take A Self-Assessment.
Go to www.capbuildermember.com and select the **Personal Development Coaching Program**.

5 Make It So

> *"Every time you are tempted to react in the same old way, ask yourself if you want to be a prisoner of the past or a pioneer of the future."*
> **Deepak Chopra**

Fact. Very few of us have ever been in control of our own mind. You might think you have been but honestly you haven't and it's not your fault. It is just the way it is. Let's break it down. From the minute, you were born someone has been conditioning and telling you what to do and how to act. Think about it. What are the first words a baby learns? Your got it, the word no. No don't do this, no don't touch this, don't say that, don't cry, no, no, no. We were told it was for our own good. Was it really for us or for the persons responsible for our well-being?

Then we start school and were taught the fundamental rules to life. 1 + 1 = 2. If a train leaving New York is traveling at 60 mph, blah, blah, blah. Dress like this, talk like that. Most important, if you don't do it this way it will not work.

We graduate school (because we are told that this is what we must do to be successful) and start a job and guess what it starts all over again. To succeed, you must make your best working hours between 8:30 am and 5 pm.

Some of us get married because living single without a wife or husband, children and mounds of debt is just not acceptable. For you to fit in you have to be like the rest of us.

For some of us the only time we feel in control is when we are drunk or high. You all have friends that once they have had a few drinks they now control everything. They say things like "I got this" or "you're not the boss of me".

Once again, I must remind you that this is not your fault. You did not stand a chance from the minute you took your first breath.

It is time you start training your old mind and create a new mind.

I say new mind because you are going to have to retire the old one. Otherwise it will continue to fight for control and after all this time it will continue to win.

How can you train the new mind with the old one still in place? The simple answer, a little at a time. Just like everything else.

The mind is just like a muscle; it needs to be trained.

Up to now someone else has trained your mind. Your parents, family, friends, employers to name a few. Think of your training your new mind the same way you train your body to lose weight or get into shape. A min of 30 minutes a day at least 5 days a week to get any type of results in a reasonable amount of time.

How many of you have worked on training your own mind? Many of us are very good at training others but how many have learned how to train yourself. Think about it, most of the time we must go to someone else to train us because we haven't learned the discipline to train ourselves.

To train ourselves we must talk to ourselves and we all have heard the expression "it is ok to talk to yourself but if you hear answers you must be crazy"

This is so far from the truth. Once again one of those rules imposed on us from birth. The truth is that if you don't talk to yourself how can you ever get to know who you are?

Find out who you are and what you want out of your life.

To find out who you are you must have a conversation with yourself daily. I don't mean a chat; I mean a real conversation.

Having the right mindset

Most successful people you meet will have one thing in common, a success mindset. It doesn't matter, a small business person, an artist, musician, or chef. They all have the mindset to get out of their own way and to see things that others cannot see.

Why are some people more successful than others? They may come from diverse backgrounds or struggles and little money yet they become very successful. It's not where you come from that determines what you can or cannot achieve. Having the right mindset, is the key factor to being successful in business and in life.

Many times, we get in our own way. Our own thoughts hold us back from succeeding. We second-guess ourselves. We have negative thoughts and tell ourselves that sometimes were not good enough, or whatever fits the situation

This is all self-sabotaging behavior…Behavior we can change.

You can find many reasons why we do this, but it doesn't matter. What matters is that this behavior needs to change.

What is mindset?

Mindset has four basic parts your intelligence, your behavior, your abilities, and skills. Your mindset is your belief about yourself and your most basic qualities. It's your belief if these are fixed traits they are things that you can't change to take more control of your life.

There are only really two types of mindset fixed mindset and growth mindset.

Fixed Mindset

People with a fixed mindset believe that they have everything they need to succeed. They believe they are guaranteed success because of what they already have. They don't try new things, take chances, or even look at things from a different point of view. They often feel that they must prove things to themselves and others. They only do things they feel comfortable doing.

Growth Mindset

People with a growth mindset believe anyone can be successful if they just work hard and have the right attitude. They don't quit and they continue to strive while others run into roadblocks.

They know there's always room for improvement and they are not afraid to fail. They are willing to put forth the massive action that moves them towards their goals.

You must develop a growth mindset to achieve your goals and objectives.

Before we began working on developing a new business idea I think it is important to have the right mindset.

> **DoThis! – Develop an Action Plan.** Go to www.capbuildermember.com and select the **Personal Development Coaching Program**.

6 To Boldly Go Where No Man Has Gone Before

> *"Mindset will change your reality and destination. Are you ready? If yes, start THINKING victory. Trust me - you will win."* – **Bobby F. Kimbrough Jr.**

Setting A Destination

Without a destination in mind we would just wander through life. Most of us have been focused on being who the world wanted us to be so naturally we were going to places that we needed to go to be those people.

Meaning that we did not have our own destination in mind we are following the destination of others. We were told to get a job, get married, buy a house, buy a car, have children, pay your bills etc. etc. etc. It is time for you to select your own destination.

It doesn't mean you have to go there by yourself. Those that are with you can come along, but it's time you start walking in your purpose.

In the book the 4 Hour Work Week written by Tim Farris (a must read) he introduces something called dream lining. This is where you start working on what you want your life to be. Here we will use a portion of this exercise to start defining our destination. I do however recommend that you read the 4 Hour Work Week and do the full exercise.

This is a very important step in creating a new life. You must make decisions now on what you want. These decisions may change later but you must make them now. Think about what you want to have, who you want to be and what you want to be doing 3 months from now.

For example, you may want to have a new computer, be a healthier cook and be doing your first 5 K race.

You will figure out what the total cost are, add them to your current expenses and divide by the number of days you will work to get how much you will need to make per day to achieve your goals.

New Computer ($750/3 Months)	$250
Cooking Class ($150/3 Months)	$50
5 K Race Registration	$25
Current Expenses Per Month	$2500
Total Monthly Expenses	$2825
Total Daily Revenue (6 days per week/192 hrs per month)	About $120 Per day or $15 per hour

This daily revenue can be a part of your already existing income from a job or other activity.

Creating Your Plan

Write down the three statements one below the other with a little space to write in between

- In 3 months, I dream of having:
- In 3 months, I dream of being:
- In 3 months, I dream of doing:

Ask these questions for each

- Is this a reasonable target goal?
- Will I need help making it happen?
- What is the very first task that I need to do each?

It is better to have a destination than to just wander. Having a destination keeps you from following someone else. Remember, if you are not controlling your time… someone else will be

7 SULU, SET PHASERS TO STUN

> *"Success? I don't know what that word means. I'm happy. But success, that goes back to what in somebody's eyes success means. For me, success is inner peace. That's a good day for me."* **Denzel Washington**

Success is not created overnight. The successful people you know have achieved their success by making daily choices about how they're going to live their life.

> *Be warned some of these changes will upset and "stun" those around you. It might take a little time before they can and willing adjust to your new behavior.* **Marc Parham**

Successful people are aware of who they are and the take their personal development very seriously. They continuously strive to make themselves better.

How often do you assess your habits? Do you look for ways to improve and celebrate your wins? If you want more successes in your life just start by changing how you conduct your day.

Take a look at a few habits you do have and maybe you don't know that they are affecting how much success you get out of each day.

You forget your strengths when things get hard

- Every day things come at us that we don't expect and sometimes we get stuck focusing on those things. You must remind yourself every day of your strengths and values. This will give you a great start to helping you develop a better solution much faster without the option of going down the rabbit hole of those unexpected activities.

You focus on the small things

- Instead of prioritizing the most important things that you need accomplish each day you focus on the small activities to feel you're getting something accomplished. You could do something as simple as deciding each morning the top three things that must be done each day. That's the only three. The thing you must get done, the thing you would like to get done, and the thing that if you get it done you've gotten a bonus for the day, you do the happy dance.

You allow energy vampires to take your time

- I bet you check your email all day long. Do you really need to check it that often? What will happen if you don't check it for two hours? I bet the world will not come to an end. How often do you have conversations with people that are not tied to achieving your daily projects or goals? Do you have to answer your phone every time it rings? I bet you the world does not come to an end if you don't.

Managing Your Time

You're going to have to learn how to manage your schedule. One question that I get asked quite a bit is how do I fit this new life that I am developing into my existing day? I say don't make it fit, create new time for it. Try getting up two hours earlier at least one or two days a week. Use that time to work on the new you. You will find that as you develop your new mind, you will start taking over time the old you that has been controlling you for a very long time.

Time Management Plan

To get better control over your time you will first have find out how you currently use it. I want you to develop a time management journal and use if for 1 to 2 weeks. Keep track of thinks like;

- The time you get up and go to sleep
- Your overall feeling about this day
- When and what you eat
- Activities that you planned
- Activities that you didn't plan

Do this for a week or two and review the outcome. I promise you will see where your time is going. I bet most of it to activities that you didn't plan.

DoThis! – Time Management Plan. Use the information above to create a time management plan for the next two weeks.

8 Warp Factor 7

> *Don't just take action, TAKE MASSIVE ACTION!*, **Marc Parham**

The biggest reason a lot of businesses never get off the ground because the people that have the business idea never take action to move the idea forward. They research it, they talk about it, but they never actually take the steps to make their dreams come true. It is time for you to put your plan into action. It is time for you to take the steps that you need to take that you have in your plan to make things happen to make your dreams come true.

Small Business Revisited

Remember when your parents, uncles, aunts, relatives, and other friends had more than one job. One of my uncles worked on cars and my grandmother did hair and other people did a variety of things to make money.

They had a main job that they did during the day or night and then had something else that they did on the weekends and other free time.

We have always been small business persons. We have always used our skills to take care of our families.

Within the last few years something has changed!

People have been told that they only need an education, a job, a house, and a car and they will be living the American dream. A dream that has been recently shattered by the current economic situation. People have done what they were told and now are losing everything that they worked so hard to get.

They worked so hard for someone else!

The same someone who when the times got hard, took the money, and literally ran.

It is time to get back to the things that made this country what it once was, people working for themselves, working together to create a safe and secure life for their families.

I want you to follow these steps:

Set a personal mission statement.

- Every entrepreneur should develop and set their own personal mission statement. Is important that you write it down and carry with you, read aloud and memorize it. Do whatever you need to do to keep it with you. It will serve as a constant reminder of what walking in your purpose as a small business owner means to you.

Start with a routine

- Sometimes getting started is the hardest part about moving forward. For this reason start every day with great morning routine. A routine that will help your mind and body be more focus and prepared to start changing your life. Develop a routine that works for you. People always ask me how do I fit more into my day? It is sometimes hard to fit more into your day. What I suggest you do is to create more day. You can easily do this by getting up 30 minutes earlier in the morning and using this time to start your new morning routine.

Make a commitment

There are generally two types of commitment. Commitment to ourselves and Commitment to others. When asked which one to we make the most, the general answer is…To others!

Why is that? Once again you have been trained this way!

You have been taught to honor the commitments made directly or indirectly to others before the ones you make to yourself. Direct commitments are the ones that you purposely agree to like raising your child. Indirect commitments are the ones that are imposed upon you that you sometimes grudging accept. You listen on the phone for two hours to a friend that is complaining about the same thing they did the last time you talked because you are committed to the friendship. Two hours gone that will never come back.

The main reason that you will accept indirect commitments is because you really don't have anything planned for the time they take. For example, that same friend calls to discuss that same 2 hour issue but now you are working on the task that you previously laid out in the last exercise. Maybe you need to do research on a business idea or a class that you want to take.

Now you can say with clear conscience that you have some work to do right now and you will reach out to them later. I also bet that when you do reach out that major problem they had no longer exist.

If you are not controlling your time and efforts, someone else is.

DoThis! – What is Your Unique Selling Proposition. Go to www.capbuildermember.com and select the **Personal Development Coaching Program.**

9 HIGHLY ILLOGICAL...

> "Insufficient facts always invite danger." - *Star Trek*, season 1, episode 24 ("Space Seed," 1968)

Start a business without a real plan...Highly Illogical

How do you come up with a business idea? I suggest you first look at yourself and find things that you like to do. Or look at a problem or concern that you want to address. Or maybe you see an existing business that you could put a new twist on the make it better. Whatever it is, it has a something that you are passionate about doing. Something you would do for no money if money were not the issue.

Every business solves a problem, that's it, it is as simple as that!

Your mission, if you decide to accept it, is to figure out what problem can you solve that people are willing to pay for.

- Think about what goods or services would improve your life

- Keep a list of your personal strengths and weaknesses in mind.

- Does anything come to mind that would improve your life?

Spend some time considering your own experiences. With some time and creativity, you can probably identify several products or services that would help you. Decide whether you'd like to provide a product or a service. A new business idea will likely either be based around a product or a service. Each requires some thought and creativity. They both have advantages and challenges that you should consider before focusing on one or the other.

Product or Service

Product

For a new product, you'll have to develop a great product or improve upon an existing one, then invest in manufacturing to produce it. This is an expense, but a successful product can be very lucrative.

Service

Providing a service will eliminate the need for developing and manufacturing a new product. However, you'll probably have to hire more people, since it will be tough to grow your business if you're the only one providing a service.

Both choices will involve marketing and advertising, so plan on investing time and money here whichever you choose.

Identify a problem with the existing industry

- Businesses or inventions often began because someone was frustrated with the current way of doing things. A great way to come up with a business idea is to look for these problems. If you're feeling frustrated about something, it is possible that others feel the same way, which gives you a potential market.

Build upon an existing business idea that works

- Rather than a problem with the current industry, you might notice something that a business does well. Take that and see if you can improve upon it. By taking ideas one step further, you can carve a good niche for yourself in the market.

Look towards the future

- Successful entrepreneurs are innovators. They don't stick with the same old methods or technologies, but rather look ahead and see what will be successful in the future. You can do this by asking yourself what the next logical step is for a product or service.

Conduct preliminary consumer research

- While market research is usually only used after you have an idea, you can do some early research to discover what people value. This can help you come up with an idea based on people's wants and needs. Search the internet and see what common keywords or internet searches are. This will show you what people search for most often, which can spark and idea for you.

Apply your skills to a different field

- Another way to come up with a new product or service is to use skills you've acquired elsewhere. Often, you can creatively apply skills learned elsewhere to improve a completely different field. When considering your business ideas, take all of your skills into account. You may have a certain talent that will revolutionize a different field.

Write down all your ideas

- Every idea, no matter how small or how seemingly pointless, could have value. Get into the habit of writing down every idea you have in a notebook, computer or a voice note. This way all your ideas can be kept in one convenient place.

Foster your creativity

- Don't be too critical of your ideas at this stage. During this brainstorming period, you shouldn't feel constrained. Free your mind and see what you come up with. There are several ways you can stimulate your creativity and help come up with ideas.

Evaluating the Business Idea

One of the most overlooked steps when thinking about starting a business is doing a true evaluation of the business idea. A lot of people that I've coached about starting a business tell me the first business they started they jumped out there started doing it. No real plan, just getting out there and making it happen. I'm certain there have been some very successful businesses that came from a start like this. I am also certain that there are many more successful businesses that take the time to truly evaluate their business idea.

It is important to get your idea out of your head and on the paper so you can look at. As long as it is in your head it just keeps moving around changing shape, changing colors and changing sizes.

When asked, most people don't thoroughly evaluate their business idea because they think that they must write a business plan. Yes, a business plan is very important but at this stage you just need to evaluate the business idea.

The Business Idea Evaluation Tool contained in this book will help you evaluate your business idea. Don't think too hard when answering the questions. Give the answer that first comes to mind. If it doesn't sound right in may be something you need to research better. The whole purpose of this exercise for you to get that information out of your head and onto paper you can see what it looks like. When you see it on paper you will be allowed also see if it makes sense.

This tool will help you evaluate the following areas;

1. The Problem
2. Who has the Problem
3. Your Solution to the Problem
4. Why You?
5. How to reach those that have the Problem
6. How much will it cost?
7. How much will I sell it for?
8. How much money can I make?
9. Is this a good business idea?

 **DoThis! – Evaluate Your Great Business Idea.** Go to www.capbuildermember.com and select the **Develop Your Business Idea**

10 I'm Givin' Her All She's Got, Captain!"

> *You may encounter many defeats, but you must not be defeated. In fact, it may be necessary to encounter the defeats, so you can know who you are, what you can rise from, how you can still come out of it,* **Maya Angelou**

It is imperative that you develop a plan for your future. Not just a business plan but a strategic plan for your life. The business will only be part of it. Without a plan, you will find yourself trying many things without success. Your plan will help stay the course. Your plan will help you minimize time, minimize your expenses, and will give you the tools to measure how successful you are.

Most of the time what is missing is for you to have a "defined" plan for your life. When I say "defined" I don't mean something that we dream or hope will happen. It must be something that we have researched, developed and documented to happen. Isn't it easier when you have a map or plan to follow when you want to get somewhere?

Let's develop a plan!

If you had a meeting with yourself 12 months from today, what will you tell yourself about your life?

Are you ready to answer a few questions about yourself and your great business idea? Are you ready to start developing a business plan?

Begin by answering the basic questions about, you, your business idea and your plan to get you where you want to be. If you have been doing the DoThis exercises you have already answered most of the questions. These tools are not pass or fail. There are only used to determine your level of comfort or knowledge about yourself and your idea. The results of these tools will be used to help get prepared to develop you and take your idea into action.

The CAPBuilder Business Plan Development Tool

This evaluation tool at the end of this book will help you to answer the basic questions about your business idea. Only answer the questions that you have the immediate answers to. Put an N/A in any area that you don't know yet. These will be the areas that you will work on with your business coach.

DoThis! –Business Plan Development Tool. Go to www.capbuildermember.com and select the **Develop Your Business Plan Coaching Program.**

11 THE FINAL FRONTIER

As you embark on this journey it is important to remember to take very loving care of your vessel. We sometimes take our vessel for granted. As long as we wake up every day and everything seems like it is working ok we never really check to see how things are really going.

Yes, when we do get sick we do take the steps necessary to fix the problem. But the truth of the matter is if we did not get sick we would probably never think to make sure everything is working correctly.

You will have to become your own engineer just like Scotty on Star Trek. He knew exactly what his ship would take. He would even sometime countermand the orders from the Captain. This is what you are going to learn that you will have to do.

My Personal Story

A few years ago I had a health scare that prompted me to change my life by becoming Vegan. This was one of the most difficult things that I had ever attempted and I did it for about 1 year. It was during this year that I learned the power of the food that I put into my body. I also learned about the physical and spiritual aspects of taking care of myself.

This sounds like I was on the correct path right?

Well I was but I slowly not only slipped back into some of my old ways I actually convinced myself that I could treat everything in my life naturally without the aid of medicine and regular health care from a Medical Doctor.

I juiced, practiced yoga, did meditation and many other things. I felt great. My body mass index (BMI) was where it was supposed to be and I always got comments on how great I looked. I even convinced myself that I did not need to pay the exorbitant cost of medical health care insurance. I even believed one of my non-western health care advisors that by living my life like this I had health assurance vs health insurance.

I could not have been farther from the truth. Last year for a couple of evenings I was having a little trouble breathing. I wrote it off to the amount of recent travel and the stress that I was under.

I decided however to go get it check out. I went into the hospital for what I thought would be a quick visit and a medical prescription and ended up staying for an entire week. It was very confusing for the doctors because the way I looked, having no other symptoms in no pain they could not figure out what was wrong.

The diagnosis totally rocked my world. I am now on medication and totally changed the way that I live my life. The scary story, had I not have gone in you might now be reading my obituary.

The Moral to This Story

Please, Please, Please get yourself checked out on a regular basis regardless of the lifestyle you have chosen.

12 SUMMARY

I have given you the information and tools to get your journey started. It is now up to you to make use of this information. You may not think you are ready or those around you keep saying you have a lot of work to do.

I say, go ahead and get started today! All you have to do is take one step at a time. Before you know it you will be farther down the road then you expected. Especially if you have utilized the tools and resources on the www.capbuildermember.com site to develop and follow a plan.

Remember I am only a click away if you need help or just want to talk. Go to www.meetwithmarc.com and schedule a coaching session. You will be glad you did!

Marc E. Parham

13 CAPBuilder Self-Assessment

This survey will ask you yes or no questions that pertain to some of the most important aspects of starting a business. This is not a pass or fail test. You will use the answer to determine what else you need to help you get started.

Pay close attention to the "No" responses. These are the ones that we will need to focus on to get you ready for business.

Please provide the following (*required)

First Name	
Last Name	
Title	
Company	
Address	
City	
State / Province	
Postal Code	
Phone	
Biz Coach Email	
Your Email	

General

1. Do you think you are ready to start a business?

   (Select only one.)
   ☐ No
   ☐ Yes

2. Have you ever worked in a business similar to what you are planning to start?

   (Select only one.)
   ☐ No
   ☐ Yes

3. Would people that know you say you are well suited to be self-employed?

   (Select only one.)
   ☐ No
   ☐ Yes

4. Do you have support for your business from family and friends?

   (Select only one.)
   ☐ No
   ☐ Yes

5. Have you ever taken a course or seminar designed to teach you how to start and manage a small business?

   (Select only one.)
   ☐ No

☐ Yes

Personal Characteristics

6. Do you consider yourself a leader and self-starter?

   (Select only one.)
   ☐ No
   ☐ Yes

7. Would other people consider you a leader?

   (Select only one.)
   ☐ No
   ☐ Yes

8. Do you have enough confidence in yourself and your abilities to sustain yourself in business, if or when things get tough?

   (Select only one.)
   ☐ No
   ☐ Yes

9. Do you like to make your own decisions?

   (Select only one.)
   ☐ No
   ☐ Yes

10. Are you prepared, if needed, to temporarily lower your standard of living until your business is firmly established?

    (Select only one.)

☐ No
☐ Yes

11. Are you willing to commit long hours to make your business work?
(Select only one.)
☐ No
☐ Yes

Skills and Experience

12. Do you have a business plan for the business you are planning to start?

(Select only one.)
☐ No
☐ Yes

13. Do you know and understand the components of a business plan?

(Select only one.)
☐ No
☐ Yes

14. Do you know what form of legal ownership (sole proprietor, partnership or corporation) is best for your business?

(Select only one.)
☐ No
☐ Yes

15. Do you know why some consider business planning to be the most important factor determining business success?

(Select only one.)
☐ No
☐ Yes

Additional Comments

16. Please tell why you feel that you are ready to start a business?

14 CAPBuilder Business Idea Evaluation Tool

Instructions

This evaluation tool will help you to determine if your business idea will be something that you consider worth doing. For some of you it may be money for others it may be something else. What is most important is that you are doing something that will be rewarding.

Follow the instructions below to evaluate your business idea.

- Only develop one idea at a time
- Use a different survey for each idea
- There are no wrong answers
- This is just a first pass at developing your idea
- You may come back and do it again
- And again

Answer questions as they relate to you. For most answers, check the boxes most applicable to you or fill in the blanks.

NOTE: Enter your Business Coaches email address where it says Biz Coach Email. If you do not have a business coach enter your email address.

Please provide the following

First Name	
Last Name	
Title	
Company	
Address	
City	
State / Province	
Postal Code	
Phone	
Biz Coach Email	
Your Email	
Website	
Facebook	
Twitter	

THE IDEA -What is the Problem that your idea is going to solve?

What are the problems that your business is going to solve?

Are these REAL problems or have you used your product to create the problem?

1. Describe the major problem that your business idea will solve. (For example: Grass needs to be cut

CUSTOMER -Who has the Problem?

- Who are the people that have the problem?
- How large is the problem for them?
- How bad do they need the problem solved?

2. Describe the person or group that has the problem. (For Example: People that can't cut their own grass)

THE PRODUCT/SERVICE -What is your solution to the Problem?

- What products or services will your business provide to solve the problem?
- Sketch out the top features or capabilities next to each problem.
- Bind a solution to your problem
    - PROBLEM:
    - SOLUTION:

3. What is your solution to the problem? (For example: I will provide grass cutting services)

UNIQUE SELLING PROPOSITION -Why can you solve this Problem?

- Why buy from you?
- What makes you and your product unique.
- Be different, but make sure your difference matters
- Focus on finished story benefits
- A good USP gets inside the head of your customers and focuses on the benefits your customers derive after using your product.

Step 1: What are your top 3 strengths? What do you offer clients that you do really well?

Step 2: How are each of your strengths better than your competition's?

Step 3: What's different about you? Look at your education, process, guarantee, offer, background, Experience, who you work with, etc.

(Provide only one response)

Step 4: For every statement you listed in Steps 1-3, ask, why they are important to your customer. What is going to motivate you customer to buy from you. Write your USP in 10 words or less

MARKETING - How will you reach those that have the Problem

- How are you going to reach and sell your products to your customers?
- Inbound versus Outbound
- Inbound channels use "pull messaging" to let customers find you organically while outbound channels rely on "push messaging" for reaching customers.
    - Example inbound channels: Blogs, SEO, E-books, white papers, webinars.
    - Example outbound channels: SEM, print/TV ads, trade shows, cold calling

How to you plan to reach your potential customers?

(Select all that apply)
☐ Internet
☐ Social Media
☐ Advertising
☐ Direct Sells
☐ Flyers
☐ Inbound Marketing
☐ Outbound Marketing
☐ Marketing Company
☐ Other:

COST - What will it cost to make or provide 1 unit of your PRODUCT/SERVICE

What are the cost to make and deliver 1 unit of your product?

- Labor -
- Materials -
- Total   -

What is the total COST OF MATERIALS used to used to provide your product or service? For example (Gas to and from the client and to cut the grass)

What is the total COST OF LABOR used to provide one unit of the product or service? (For example - I will pay $10 an hour to cut a yard. 1 hour estimated to cut one yard)

TOTAL COST - Add the MATERIAL COST + LABOR COST enter the TOTAL COST

PRICE - What will you sell your 1 unit of your PRODUCT/SERVICE

What are you going to charge for 1 unit of your product?

- Price -
- Cost -
- Net -

Cost - Please enter the total cost from question 6

Enter the price that you want to sell your product or service for. (For example - I will charge $40 to cut the average yard.)

NET PROFIT - Subtract the cost from the price and enter the net profit. The money that is made after you pay the cost for the product or service. (For example - $40 Price - $15 Total Cost ($10 labor, $5 Gas) = $25 Net Revenue)

PROJECTIONS -How many of your PRODUCT/SERVICE can you sell in a MONTH

What will be the gross revenue target per month

- Qty Per Wk -   X
- 4 Wks =   X
- Price   = Gross Monthly Revenue
- _____

WEEKLY UNITS SOLD - How many units can you sell in 1 week? (For example - How many yards can I cut in 1 week?)

MONTHLY UNITS SOLD - How many units can you sell in 1 month? Multiply Units Sold Per Week x 4 and enter the total? (For example - 25 Yards cut per week x 4 = 100 yards per month)

GROSS MONTHLY REVENUE - How much GROSS REVENUE can you make per month? Multiply MONTHLY UNITS SOLD x PRICE PER UNIT = GROSS MONTHLY REVENUE (For example - 100 Yards per month X $40 Per yard = $4000)

TOTAL YEARLY GROSS REVENUE - How much estimated revenue can I generate in 1 year? Multiple TOTAL MONTHLY GROSS REVENUE x 12 MONTHS = YEARLY ESTIMATE REVENUE.

This is only an estimate. Your business may have cycles or seasons. (For example - $4000 GROSS REVENUE PER MONTH X 12 MONTHS = $48,000 YEARLY ESTIMATED REVENUE)

IDEA EVALUATION

Please answer the following questions to evaluate if this business idea will work for you at this time. Sometimes we have great ideas but it may not be the time for them. If you answered NO to any of the questions this idea my not work for you right now. You may need to go back and do the survey again or try another approach.

Does this still seem like a great business idea?

　☐Yes
　☐No

Can I make money with this business idea? Want to make sure that you are making more than you are spending.

　☐Yes
　☐No

Am I willing to put in the time to make this work?

　☐Yes
　☐No

Am I ready to do the research and write the business plan for this idea?

☐ Yes
☐ No

SUMMARY

Please enter any comments or thoughts on this business idea?

15 CAPBuilder Coaching Programs

I have developed a number of great coaching programs that will help you to start or grow your business. The great thing about these programs is that they can all be done online at your own pace with or without a business coach. Each coaching program contains access to the tools and resources that you will need to successfully complete the program.

Basic program components;

- Workshop Presentation – There will be a workshop presentation that I have successfully used while doing group training that you can view that will give an overview of the program topic.

- Tools and Assessments – There will be a list of recommended online tools and assessments that you will use that will ask you questions to help you develop your plan. If you select the 1 on 1 coaching option, your coach will use the results of the tools to assist you with your plan development.

- Links to Resources – There will be links to additional resources including podcast, articles and videos that you will also use to develop your plan.

How it works

Go to the www.capbuildemember.com site and select Coaching Programs to view and register for the coaching program you need.

Our Virtual Coaching Programs

- We will coach you on the phone or online video conference!
- We will coach you when you are available!
- We will coach you to stay focused on your goals!

Self-paced Coaching

- Sign up for your **FREE** membership
- Select the **FREE** coaching program that meets your needs.
- Follow the instructions
- **Pay as you go for coaching sessions**

Group Coaching

- Sign up for your **FREE** membership
- Select the **PAID** coaching program that meets your needs.
- **You will receive a schedule of the online webinars associated with your coaching program**

1 on 1 Coaching

- Sign up for your **FREE** membership

- Select the **PAID** coaching program that meets your needs.

- You will receive a FREE introductory coaching session with a business coach that will go over the program and develop your coaching session schedule.

- You will receive a schedule of the online webinars associated with your coaching program.

16 About the Author

Marc E. Parham Bio

Marc E. Parham is a small business expert, professional speaker, radio host and author of the book "**Yes I Can – Develop My Idea and Start My Own Business**". He has been working for over 20 years to help people start and grow businesses.

His mission is simple, to educate and coach people to start taking more control of their lives by learning how to start their own small business.

Marc is a Managing Partner at the CAPBuilder Network Group; (www.capbuildernetwork.com) a consulting company whose focus is helping people start and grow their own businesses. He is the creator the successful business information site called The CapBuilder Network (www.capbuildernetwork.com) and radio talk show CAPBuilder Talk (www.capbuildertalk.com) that provides articles, information and resources to help start and grow small businesses. He also the director of Entrepreneurship at the Urban League of Greater Atlanta.

On October 11, 2013 Marc was invited and attended a meeting with President Obama to discuss how the shut down and debt ceiling issues were affecting small business. The meeting was held at the White House and it was co-sponsored by Business Forward. Marc, a member of the Business Forward Local Leadership Council was one of a select group of nine individuals invited to attend the meeting.

He is available for speaking, coaching and other business events using the contact information listed below.

email: marcp@capbuildernetwork.com 770-634-7231

Website: www.marceparham.com, www.capbuildernetwork.com, www.capbuildertak.com

17 CAPBUILDER RESOURCE PAGE

SITE LINK	SITE DESCRIIPTION
www.marcparham.com	Media kit and other information on Marc Parham
www.capbuildernetwork.com	Main CAPBuilder Network Site. Go to this site to access all tools and resources.
www.capbuildertalk.com	Listen to the CAPBuilder Talk radio show hosted by Marc Parham
www.capbuildercoaching.com	Register to take one of the great coaching programs self paced or with a business coach.
www.capbuildernews.com	News blog about small business, community and health.
www.capbuilderradionetwork.com	Listen to great radio shows
www.capbuildermember.com	Membershiip site for the CAPBuilder Network

www.ingramcontent.com/pod-product-compliance
Lightning Source LLC
Chambersburg PA
CBHW070135210526
45170CB00013B/1089